Karl Marx
EVENING HOUR
Poems

Selected, translated & introduced by
Philip Wilson

Edited by
Jean Boase-Beier

2022

Published by Arc Publications,
Nanholme Mill, Shaw Wood Road
Todmorden OL14 6DA, UK
www.arcpublications.co.uk

978 1911469 09 4

Design by Tony Ward
Printed in the UK by ImprintDigital.com

ACKNOWLEDGEMENTS
The translator would like to thank Davide Rizza, who first introduced him to Marx's verse, and Helen Tierney, who persuaded him to translate 'Evening Hour' for a Highgate poetry walk. His thanks also go to Arc Publications' Tony Ward and Angela Jarman who are as ever good to work with, and to Jean Boase-Beier for editing this volume with her customary expertise. The following have also been generous with their support: Birgit Breidenbach, Marc Fielder, Tom Greaves, Gareth Jones, Duncan Large, Kate Lawton, Silvia Caprioglio Panizza and Holly Purdham.

The source texts are taken from: Marx, K. (1975) *Werke, Artikel, Literarische Versuche bis März 1843*, Berlin: Dietz. Some spellings differ from contemporary German.

Arc Chapbook Series
Series Editor: Tony Ward

CONTENTS

INTRODUCTION: MARX THE POET?

Karl Marx is remembered for creating a political philosophy that inspired revolutionaries across the globe. Marx's biographer Francis Wheen notes that within one hundred years of Marx's death, half the world's population was governed by regimes that claimed to follow his teachings.[1] Marx's works, including those co-authored with Friedrich Engels, run to fifty volumes and continue to be studied. However, things could have been very different.

Born in Trier in the Rhineland in 1818, Marx developed a love of both German and World Literature while at grammar school. He proceeded to Bonn University in 1835 as a student of jurisprudence, one year later transferring to Berlin. The young Marx dreamed of a career as a man of letters. He wrote poetry prolifically for two years, hoped to publish his work and compiled one handwritten album to his father and three to Jenny von Westphalen, whom he was to marry in 1843. He worked on a novel *Scorpion and Felix* and a verse tragedy *Oulamen*. He considered writing Platonic dialogues. By 1841, however, Marx had come to the conclusion that he lacked the talent to pursue a literary vocation. He wrote to his father that he regarded his verse as "nothing natural, everything built out of moonshine, complete opposition between what is and what ought to be, rhetorical reflections instead of poetic thought, but perhaps also a certain warmth of feeling and striving for poetic fire".[2] In later years he would laugh about his work. His final engagement with lyric poetry was in 1839, when he created a fourth album for Jenny, but copied out folk songs from a wide range of traditions rather than using his own writings. The poet was no more. Marx also abandoned the law and dedicated the

[1] Wheen, F. *Karl Marx*, London: Fourth Estate (1999), p. 1.

[2] Marx, K. and F. Engels, *Collected Works Volume One, Karl Marx: 1835-43*, tr. by R. Dixon, C. Dutt, J. Lindsay, A. Miller, D. J. and S. R. Struick, A. West, London: Lawrence and Wishart (1975), p. 11.

rest of his life to political theory and practice, following his dictum in the eleventh of the *Theses on Feuerbach* that philosophers should not interpret the world but change it. He led a wandering, stateless life that took him to Paris, Brussels, back to his homeland to encourage the uprisings of 1848, and finally to London. He supported himself and his family – he and Jenny had six children – through journalism but was frequently in financial trouble and forced to rely on others, particularly Engels.

A surprising amount of the verse written in 1836-7 has survived, some 120 poems, many of which are sequences. There are ballads, satires, epigrams, translation from Ovid's Latin, occasional poems and love lyrics. The verse comes across as very competent pastiche: the ballads and the love lyrics ventriloquise Friedrich von Schiller and Heinrich Heine respectively, for example. Marx's poetic output has attracted relatively little attention. Why read it today, then, either in German or in translation?

It is always interesting to discover that a major thinker has written poems. We can today read the verse of Mao Zedong, Iris Murdoch, Friedrich Nietzsche, Simone Weil and even a comic poem by Ludwig Wittgenstein. To encounter Marx's poems is at the very least to realise how his philosophical work came to incorporate so many literary tropes. Gareth Stedman Jones remarks that the phrases of *The Communist Manifesto* "have resonated in literature and the political imagination long after the disappearance of the circumstances which originally brought them into being".[3] It opens with the image of Europe haunted by the spectre of communism and ends with the assertion that the proletarians have nothing to lose but their chains and a world to win. Both the style and the content of Marx's later writings can be viewed as having origins in the verse.[4]

[3] Jones, G. S. *Karl Marx: Greatness and Illusion*, London: Penguin (2016), p. 241.
[4] Johnston, W. M. "Karl Marx's Verse of 1836-1837 as a Foreshadowing of his Early Philosophy", in *Journal of the History of Ideas*, Vol. 28, No. 2, (1967) pp. 259-268.

With the collapse of communist regimes in Eastern Europe in the late twentieth century, statues and images of Marx were destroyed in waves of protest. The extent of the crimes against humanity perpetrated by so-called Marxists was also by now apparent. To read Marx's poems is, however, to be taken back to a time when a young man from Trier was trying to find his way in a volatile world and was falling in love. It is to be given a unique insight into one of history's great thinkers at a time when it is urgent to re-evaluate Marx after Marxism, to look past the myths that have been constructed about the man and his work and to see what he still has to say to us in our present time of crisis. The poems offer a window onto a philosopher and his age and can help in this task. They may be full of the poetic currency of the day, but it was a currency that Marx actively chose to adopt, as the scholar S. S. Prawer argues.[5]

Arc Publications has pioneered the enlightened practice of placing source texts opposite target texts in the many translations that they issue. The reader is therefore able to see what is going on in the source language, even if this amounts only to picking out key words or noting the shape of a poem. What will immediately be apparent is how tightly structured Marx's verse is. It uses received forms (such as the sonnet or the quatrain), is rhythmically patterned and usually relies on full rhyme. Marx, a philosopher who looked to the future, had a strong sense of tradition. I have attempted to suggest this formalism in translation, because it is so integral to the work. To give three examples: I maintain the presence of rhyme, often through pararhyme; I imitate the rhythm of the unrhymed classical satires; I use an English ballad meter for the ballad of the two harp-singers. I agree with poet and translator David Constantine that the language of poetry both in source text and translation should carry with it some feeling of "coming from abroad".[6]

[5] Prawer, S. S. *Karl Marx and World Literature*, Oxford: Oxford University Press (1976), p.18.
[6] Constantine, D. *A Living Language*, Newcastle: Bloodaxe (2004), p. 24.

A chapbook can make no claim to completeness. I have chosen poems that have drawn critical attention, that are not too long and that I happen to like because they genuinely burn with the "poetic fire" for which Marx strove. I have ordered them thematically rather than chronologically: verse within the German tradition; poems to Jenny; satire. Each translation is prefaced by a brief note about the poem. My hope in producing *Evening Hour* is that readers will be introduced to new aspects of Marx. To read his poems is also to evaluate his relationship with literature in general, a relationship that lasted after he had given up writing verse. His daughter Eleanor remembered him as a great storyteller, and he continued to read widely for pleasure and to use literature to shape his philosophical writings. At a family parlour game of 'Confessions' in 1865, he recorded that his favourite occupation was "book-worming" and that his favourite poets were "Shakespeare, Aeschylus, Goethe". Even at the end of his life, when illness forced him to abandon work, he was reading comic novels.

Marx died in 1883 of bronchitis and was buried in Highgate Cemetery. Engels told the small group of mourners that his friend's name and work would endure throughout the ages. As Wheen comments: "It seemed an unlikely boast, but he was right".[7]

Philip Wilson

[7] Wheen, F., *op. cit.*, p. 1.

EVENING HOUR

Poems

DICHTUNG (1837)

Schöpferähnlich strömten Flammen
Rieselnd mir aus Deiner Brust,
Hochweit schlugen sie zusammen,
Und ich nährt' sie in der Brust.
Strahlend stand Dein Bild, wie Aeolsklingen,
Deckt die Gluthen sanft mit Liebesschwingen.

Rauschen hört' ich's, sah es blinken,
Ferne Himmel zogen hin,
Tauchten auf, hinabzusinken,
Sanken, höher aufzufliehn.
Als der inn're Kampf sich nun geschlichtet,
Blickt' ich Schmerz und Lust im Lied verdichtet.

Schmiegend an der Formen Milde,
Steht die Seele festgebannt,
Aus mir schwollen die Gebilde,
Aus Dir waren sie entbrannt.
Geistig lösen sie die Liebesglieder,
Sprühn sie voll im Schöpferbusen wieder.

POETRY

One of two dedicatory lyrics to his father, the Trier lawyer Heinrich Marx, this poem explores poetic inspiration itself. Marx wanted a career that would benefit humanity and that would also complete him as a person. He thus typifies the German intellectual tradition after Goethe. The German noun "Dichtung" (poetry) is related to the verb "dichten" (to thicken) and Marx plays on etymology by his use of "verdichten" (to compress, heighten) in the second stanza. The spirit of Prometheus, the rebellious Titan who steals fire for humanity, hovers over this poem and many others.[8]

Creator-like the flames were streaming,
Pouring from within your breast,
High and wide they came together,
And I fed them in my breast.
Your radiant form, like Aeolian sound,
Covered my passions with soft wings of love.

I heard the rush, I saw the sparkle,
Distant skies now came up close,
Rose on high and then were sinking,
Sank until again they rose.
When the inner strife had died away,
I saw in song the heightened pain and joy.

Nestling in the forms so gentle –
See, the soul stands paralysed.
Deep within, each image prospered –
Your fire made them come alive.
They loosen the links of love in spirit,
And spark again in their creator's heart.

[8] Prawer, *op. cit.*, p. 31.

SPIELMANN

Spielmann streicht die Geigen,
Die lichtbraun Haare sich neigen,
Trägt einen Säbel an der Seit',
Trägt ein zerrissen gefaltet Kleid.

"Spielmann, Spielmann, was streichst du so sehr,
Spielmann, was blickst du so wild umher?
Was kreist sich das Blut, was springen die Wogen,
Zerreißt dir ja deinen Bogen."

"Was geig' ich Mensch! was brausen Wellen?
Daß donnernd sie am Fels zerschellen,
Daß's Auge erblind't, daß der Busen springt,
Daß die Seele hinab zur Hölle klingt!"

"Spielmann, zerreibst dir's Herz mit Spott,
Die Kunst, die lieh dir ein lichter Gott,
Sollst ziehn, sollst sprühn auf Klangeswellen,
Zum Sternentanz hinanzuschwellen!"

"Was, was! Ich stech', stech' ohne Fehler
Blutsschwarz den Säbel in deine Seele,
Fort aus dem Haus, fort aus dem Blick,
Willst Kindlein spielen um dein Genick?

Gott kennt sie nicht, Gott acht't nicht die Kunst,
Die stieß in den Kopf aus Höllendunst,
Bis das Hirn vernarrt, bis das Herz verwandelt,
Die hab' ich lebendig vom Schwarzen erhandelt!

MINSTREL

This poem is one of two that Marx published. The armed minstrel is a standard character of German Romanticism, embodying both the beauty and the terror of art. In Marx's poem he is an alienated figure, prepared to kill his listener. William M. Johnston interprets him as a revolutionary waiting to be born.[9]

Minstrel bows the strings.
His light brown hair hangs down.
He has a sabre by his side.
He wears a torn and pleated robe.

"Minstrel, minstrel, why play so hard?
Minstrel, why is your look so wild?
Why does blood leap? Why does it flow?
It will soon tear your bow in two."

"Why do I play! Well, why do waves roar?
To shatter in thunder on the shore!
To make eyes blind! To make the heart swell!
To make the soul play itself down to hell!"

"Minstrel, your mockery crushes your heart,
But your craft was granted by some bright god,
And you must go glisten on sound's own waves,
And strive up to the dance of the stars!"

"What's that? I shall thrust, thrust without fail
My sabre, black-blooded, into your soul.
Get out of this house and out of my sight,
Unless, you child, you'd wager your neck!

God does not care, God does not know art,
Which thrust in my head from hell's own mist,
When the brain goes mad and the heart turns bad,
Things that I learned from the Prince of the Night.

[9] Johnston, *op. cit.*, p. 267.

Der schlägt mir den Takt, der kreidet die Zeichen;
Muß voller, toller den Todmarsch streichen,
Muß spielen dunkel, muß spielen licht,
Bis Herz durch Sait' und Bogen bricht."

Spielmann streicht die Geigen,
Die lichtbraun Haare sich neigen,
Trägt einen Säbel an der Seit',
Trägt ein zerrissen gefaltet Kleid.

DIE BEIDEN HARFENSÄNGERINNEN

Ballade

"Was treibt dich her zu diesem Schlosse,
Zu hauchen tiefen Gluthgesang?
Weilt dir daselbst ein Liebgenosse,
Zieht er dich her im Seelendrang?"

"Kennst du ihn, der seelenvoll hier wohnet,
Fragst mich, ob ich ihm entbrannt?
Hat sein Anblick Ird'sche je belohnet,
Die die Sehnsucht hergesandt?

Nimmer hab' ich ihn im Glanz geschauet,
Doch der Edelsteine Glühn,
Die das Prachtgebäude stolz erbauet,
Mußten wohl mich herwärts ziehn.

Denn es ist, als wär' ich hier geboren,
Hier mein heimathliches Land;
Ach! es steht vom weichem Süd erkoren,
Wie des Himmels Erdenland.

He beats out my rhythm and chalks out the score,
And faster and faster the death march I draw,
Must play the dark, must play the light,
Till string and bow will break this heart."

Minstrel bows the strings.
His light brown hair hangs down.
He has a sabre by his side.
He wears a torn and pleated robe.

THE TWO HARP-SINGERS
Ballad

Two mysterious women – the German noun "Harfensängerinnen" is feminine plural – star in a ballad that reworks tropes from German legend. Marx was fond of using dialogue to structure his poems.

"What drives you to this castle, then,
To breathe deep passion's song?
Is it some lover from the past,
Whose soul has made you long?"

"You know the one whose soul lives here?
You ask if my love burned?
Did ever mortal catch his eye,
For whom such loving yearned?

I never saw him in the light,
But jewels shine so clear
Upon these proud and splendid halls
And they have drawn me here.

I feel this is my place of birth,
Yes, this my native land.
Blessed by the gentle southern wind,
It could be heaven's land.

Hier erklingen meine Lieder freier,
Schwillet höher mir die Brust,
Tönt das süsse Spiel der gold'nen Leier,
Wie von selbst in Wehmuthslust.

Und ich kenne nicht den hohen Meister,
Der in's Herz gewaltig schlägt,
Kenne nicht die zarten Himmelgeister,
Die das Schloß im Schooße trägt!

Und vergeblich ist mein heisses Sehnen,
Nimmer öffnet sich die Pforte hold,
Und ich muß mich an die Pfeiler lehnen,
Und hier singen Minnesold."

Und sie schüttelt ihre schwarzen Locken,
Strömt sich aus in Thränenflut,
Und die and're küßt die Wange trocken,
Preßt sie heiß an Busens Glut.

"Mich ziehen auch geheime Bande,
Zu diesem heil'gen Göttersitz,
Ich sucht' ihn wallend durch die Lande,
Und fernher schlug's in mich, wie Blitz.

Doch sollen bange Tränen fließen,
Warum der heiße Wehmuthstau?
Wir dürfen ja das Bild geniessen,
Und hüpfen in der Blumenau.

Der Busen darf uns voller glühen,
Der Wehmuth Schauer süsser nahn,
Die Blicke dürfen heller sprühen,
Das Schönste ist hier bald gethan.

Drum laß uns eine Hütte zielen,
Drin klinge unser Weihgesang,
Die mag der süsse West umspielen,
Und tiefverborg'ner Geisterdrang."

My songs are freer here to sing,
My heart swells in my breast.
The golden lyre plays itself
At sadness's behest.

The Master is unknown to me,
Whose heart beats to my own.
I do not know sweet heaven's ghosts
Within the castle's womb!

My longing is too hot, in vain.
The gate stands closed above.
On columns I am forced to lean,
To sing the cost of love."

And so she shakes her raven locks.
A flood of tears can start.
The other dries them with a kiss
And warms her on her heart.

"Such secret bonds have also drawn
Me here, where high gods dwell.
I sought him, pilgrim through the land.
Like lightning was his spell.

But why should melancholy's dew
In fickle tears fall down?
For we may also love this scene
And dance the meadows' bloom.

The heart can burn more fully now,
Sad shudders turn to sweet.
Our vision can fly brighter yet,
For beauty's ours to meet.

Let's find a cottage as our home.
Our sacred songs we'll sing.
The sweet west wind will play for us
And spirits hid within."

Sie weilten hier noch lange Tage,
Und Abends klingt ihr Saitenspiel,
Das lockt mit holder Wehmuthsklage,
Der Vögelein und Blüthen viel.

Und einst vom Schlummer tief durchdrungen,
In süssem Bett von weichem Moos,
Die Arm' um zarten Leib geschlungen,
Erschien ein Dämon zart und groß.

Er trägt sie fort auf gold'nen Schwingen,
Wo's sie wie Zauberfessel band,
Und Töne wunderlich erklingen,
Wo einst die stille Hütte stand.

LIED AN DIE STERNE

Es tanzen eure Reigen
In Schimmer und in Strahl,
Und eure Bilder steigen,
Und schwellen ohne Zahl.

Hier bricht die schönste Seele,
Hier springt das vollste Herz,
Und gleich 'nem Goldjuwele
Umfaßt es Todtesschmerz.

For days they stayed, for many days.
Their evening harp was heard.
It tempted with its pure lament
The flowers and the birds.

And once, as slumber claimed them both
Upon sweet moss's bed,
Each arm round tender body wrapped –
A tender Demon trod.

He bears them high on golden wing,
Bound in a magic chain,
And wondrous sounds may still be heard
Where once their cottage lay.

SONG TO THE STARS

A poem that laments the stars' lack of emotion and anticipates Marx's eventual turn against Romanticism. Truth is to be found here and now, not written in the sky. (He famously called religion the opium of the people.) Duncan Large suggests that the poem's German title may be a play on the name of Laurence Sterne, author of Tristram Shandy, *on which Marx's comic novel* Scorpion and Felix *is modelled.*[10]

You stars above are dancing,
In bright and gleaming rows.
Your image is arising,
In numbers no one knows.

The fairest spirit breaks here,
The fullest heart has leapt,
And like a golden jewel
The pain of death is kept.

[10] Large, D., "Karl Marx and Shandean Humour: *Scorpion und Felix* and its Aftermath", in K. Vieweg, J. Vigus and K.M. Wheeler, *Shandean Humour in English and German Literature and Philosophy*, London: Routledge (2013), p. 113.

Es hebt zu euch die Augen,
Mit dunkler Allgewalt,
Und will da Hoffnung saugen
Und Ewigkeitsgehalt.

Doch ach! ihr glüht nur immer,
In ruh'gem Ätherschein,
Und Götter werfen nimmer
Die Gluth in euch hinein.

Ihr seid nur Truggebilde,
Von Strahlen flammt's Gesicht,
Doch Herzensgluth und Milde,
Und Seele habt ihr nicht.

Und euer Schein ist Höhnen,
Für That und Schmerz und Drang;
An euch zerschellt das Sehnen,
Und Busens Flammensang.

Wir müssen in Leid ergrauen,
Verzweifelnd untergehn,
Und dann zum Hohne schauen,
Daß Erd' und Himmel stehn;

Daß, wenn wir auch zersplittern,
'ne Welt in uns ertrinkt,
Kein Baumstamm muß zersplittern,
Kein Stern herunter sinkt.

Sonst lägt ihr all begraben
Im tiefen blauen Meer,
Würd't keine Strahlen haben,
Und längst kein Feuer mehr.

Dann sprächt ihr stumm die Wahrheit,
Und lögt nicht todte Pracht,
Und prangtet nicht in Klarheit,
Und ringsum wär' es Nacht.

Our eyes are looking upwards
With dark eternal force.
We hope to suck down promise,
Eternity's own source.

Alas, it is just gleaming,
Just peaceful aether's glow.
The gods will never ever
Give stars the heat they know.

Your image is deception.
A fire may frame your face,
But heat of heart, and kindness,
And soul? I find no trace.

Your light just serves to mock us,
Our deeds, our pain, our stress.
You shatter all our longing,
Flame's song within the breast.

We turn to grey in sorrow,
We sink within despair,
And then see how you mock us:
That earth and sky are there;

But even if we shatter,
And all our world must drown,
No tree will ever splinter,
No star will tumble down.

For then you would be buried
Within the deep blue sea,
Then you would have no radiance:
No fire would burn for me.

And you would tell the truth then,
And not this dead delight.
You would not gleam so brightly:
Around you would be night.

AN JENNY
Sonnette

I

Jenny! spöttelnd wirst Du wohl mich fragen,
Was mein Lied sich stets: "an Jenny" nennt,
Da doch alle Pulse Dir nur schlagen,
Alle meine Lieder Dir nur klagen,
Alle Dich an ihrem Busen tragen,
Da doch jede Sylbe dich bekennt,
Jeder Ton für Dich melodisch brennt,
Und kein Hauch sich von der Göttin trennt?
Doch so süß ist mir des Namens Schallen,
Und aus seinen Zügen schlägt so viel,
Und er tönt so voll durch alle Hallen,
Trifft mich, gleich wie fernes Geisterbeben,
Wie ein Goldbesaitet Zytherspiel,
Wie ein eigen, zauberhaftes Leben.

II

Sieh! ich könnte tausend Bücher füllen,
Und nur "Jenny" schrieb ich stets hinein,
Und doch würden sie Gedanken hüllen,
Ew'ge That, unwandelbaren Willen,
Süsse Dichtung, zartes Sehnsuchtsstillen,
Alle Gluth und allen Aetherschein,
Alle Götterlust und Wehmuthspein,
All mein Wissen und mein eigen Sein.
In den Sternen kann ich ihn nur lesen,

TO JENNY
Sonnets

Marx wrote many poems to and for Jenny von Westphalen (1814-1881), from whom he was often separated before they married. Jenny was an intellectual in her own right, tutored by her father. She shared Marx's radical views, prepared his almost indecipherable manuscripts for publication and towards the end of her life wrote drama criticism for the German press. She lamented, however, that radical men could lead a public life, while their wives had to remain at home darning socks.

I

Jenny! You mock me as you question
Why my song is always called "To Jenny",
Why every pulse carries only your name,
And why you are my verse's one lament;
Why you alone are carried in my bosom,
Why syllables confess your name to me,
Why every tone proclaims your melody,
No breath to part you from divinity?
You see, your name is just the sweetest sound.
And everything is said when it is told.
It resonates through halls and all around.
It strikes me like the sound of distant ghosts.
Or like a cittern where the strings are gold.
Or like a life that's truly magical.

II

You see, a thousand volumes could be filled,
With "Jenny" as the only word I'd write,
And yet my thoughts would still remain concealed:
The eternal deed, the unchangeable will,
The sweetest verse, and longing's tender goal,
All gleam and all aethereal light,
All godly joy and melancholy's plight,
And all my knowledge, all my life.
Your name is spelled in the starry sky.

Aus dem Zephyr tönt er mir zurück,
Aus der Welle Rauscherfülltem Wesen,
Und ich denk' ihn einst in solchen Bann zu schreiben,
Daß Jahrhunderte erschaut sein Blick,
Jenny soll der Liebe Nahme bleiben.

SCHLUSSSONNETTE AN JENNY

I

So nimm sie hin, die Lieder alle,
Die Liebe Dir zu Füssen legt,
Wo frei in vollem Lyraschalle
Der Seele Gluth sich hinbewegt.
O! wenn von ihrem Widerhalle
Dein Busen sehnend aufgeregt,
Dein Puls in rasch'rem Lauf und Falle
An's hehre Herz gewaltig schlägt,

Dann tönt's zu mir aus jenen Weiten,
Wo leicht Dich trägt Dein Siegesgang.
Dann darf ich kühner ringen, streiten,
Dann klingt mein Lied verklärt und freier,
Dann wagt sich höher mein Gesang,
Dann weint vor Wehmuth meine Leier.

Your name is echoed by the west wind,
And by each wave that surges in the sea.
And I shall write it like a magic charm.
Across the centuries, your name shall not be dimmed.
The name of love is Jenny. That remains.

CONCLUDING SONNETS TO JENNY

Two of a series of four "concluding sonnets" from the first album to Jenny. Wheen asks why a woman from the Prussian ruling class and the daughter of a baron should have fallen for "a bourgeois Jewish scallywag four years her junior" and concludes that she was swayed by his "intellectual swagger".[11] The love poems must also have helped.

I

So take them, then, take every song
That love has placed before your feet,
Where free within the lyre's tone
The fire within the soul is moved.
Ah, if only from my singing's echo
Would come a longing in your breast,
A pulse that quickens, rises, falls,
Beating to your noble heart –

Then I shall hear a sound from far away,
Where soft you bear your victor's tread!
Then I shall struggle, fight more boldly,
Then my song is transfigured and free,
Then my voice moves on to higher flight.
Then with sadness see my lyre weep.

[11] Wheen, *op. cit.*, p. 17.

II

Mir kann kein Erdenruhm gewähren,
Der weit durch Land und Menschen dringt,
Den frohbesieget alle nähren,
Wenn's bebend weiter durch sie klingt,
Was Deine Blicke, wenn sie sich verklären,
Dein Herz, wenn's warm die Gluth umschlingt,
Was nur zwei tiefbewegte Zähren,
Die mein Gesang dem Aug' entringt.

Und gern verhaucht' ich alle Geister
Dahin im tiefen Lyraton,
Und fühlte sterbend mich als Meister,
Könnt' ich dieß höchste Ziel erreichen,
Erringen diesen schönsten Lohn,
Von Lust und Schmerz Dich zu erweichen.

HARMONIE

An Jenny

Kennst Du das süsse Zauberbild,
Wo Seelen ineinander fliessen,
In einem Hauche sich ergiessen,
Melodisch voll und freundlich mild?

Sie glühen auf in einer Purpurrose,
Und bergen sich verschämt im weichen Moose.

Und walle weit durch Flur und Land,
Das Zauberbild wirst Du nicht finden,
Kein Talisman vermag's zu binden,
Und keine Sonne je es fand.

II

No fame on earth could ever offer me –
Even if it conquers land and soul,
Nourishing a joyful victory,
Even if its echoes fill the world –
What your gaze, transfigured, can set free,
What your heart can offer in its glow,
What two tears can promise from the deep,
Tears that my own song has caused to flow.

And I'd be glad to breathe my final breath
Into the depth of this, my lyre's sound,
And I should feel a Master in my death,
If only I could reach this highest goal,
If only I could win this fair reward:
To soften joy and pain within your soul.

HARMONY

To Jenny

Love can overcome every obstacle. Marx and Jenny would stay together in spite of exile, illness, financial difficulties and other problems, such as Marx fathering a child by the family maid when they lived in London.

Do you know the magic fulness,
When souls flow out to meet each other,
And pour themselves in exhalation,
In melody and friendliness?

They set on fire like a purple rose
And hide themselves, ashamed, within soft moss.

And if you cross the field and meadow,
This magic fulness won't be found.
No talisman can keep it bound,
No light of sun has made it known.

Es ist in ihrem Scheine nicht entsprossen,
Hat keine Erdennahrung je genossen.

Drum bleibt es ewig prangend stehn,
Ob schwingt die Zeit den raschen Flügel,
Apollo faßt der Rosse Zügel,
Und Welten stumm im Nichts vergehn.

In sich hat's eine Kraft sich selbst erzeuget,
Die keine Welt, die selbst kein Gott ihm beuget.

Es ähnelt wohl dem Zytherklang,
Gespielt auf einer ew'gen Leier,
In stetem Glühen, steter Feier,
In hohem, sehnsuchtsvollem Drang.

O! horch den Saiten, die in Dir erschallen,
Zu suchen wird Dein Fuß nicht weiter wallen.

KLAGE

So muß ich nichtig ringen
Im heissen Seelenstreit,
Zu Dir hinanzudringen,
Von Fesseln kühn befreit.

Mir wird kein Liebeszeigen,
Kein einzig, gütig Wort,
Und Deine Lippen schweigen,
Und meine Gluth brennt fort.

Its glorious light has never seen birth.
It lacks all the nourishment of earth.

And therefore let it stay resplendent,
Even if Time beats hasty wings,
Or if Apollo clasps the reins,
And worlds go mute in nothingness.

Within itself a power has been made
That's far beyond the reach of world or God.

It seems to be the cittern's sound
That's played on an eternal lyre,
In endless and in solemn fire,
A high and yearning, longing tone.

Ah, listen to these strings reverberate,
And then your foot will cease its pilgrimage.

LAMENT

A love-poem that presents the ancient theme of the excluded lover. Alienation is an important theme in Marx's philosophy and the image of shackles will be applied to political struggle.

I'm wrestling and I'm losing,
In strife that sears my soul.
I seek to bring you closer,
To lose this shackled role.

No sign of love is coming,
No single, kindly word.
Your lips pronounce no loving.
The fire within still burns,

Bis sie im Nichts verrauchet,
So unbefriedigt leer,
Bis ich den Geist verhauchet,
Der einst so Liebehehr.

Und meiner Seele Zweige,
Sie streben nichtig auf,
In luft'gem Aetherreiche
Zu enden ihren Lauf.

Vergebens will ich saugen,
Von oben Licht und Gluth;
Du wendest weg die Augen,
Und mir entsinkt der Muth.

ABENDSTUNDE

Die Lampe brennt so stille,
Und wirft mir milden Schein,
Sie scheint mit mir zu klagen,
Als kennt' sie meine Pein.

Sie sieht mich stets so einsam,
In meine Brust versenkt,
Wenn tiefe Geistgestalten
Die Phantasie erdenkt.

Sie scheinet selbst zu ahnen,
Daß ihr armflackernd Licht
Vor einer Gluth versinket,
Die aus dem Busen bricht.

Yet soon will turn to nothing,
So unfulfilled and null,
Until my soul is fading,
Where love had once been full.

And so my spirit's branches
Strive upwards to no gain.
The airy realm of aether
Is what they hope to claim,

But it's in vain, this yearning
To suck down heaven's rays;
Your gaze is turned away now,
And all my courage fades.

EVENING HOUR

Another Romantic lyric reminiscent of Heine. Buch der Lieder *(Book of Songs) was the title of one of the three albums that Marx presented to Jenny, taking its title from the 1827 collection that made Heine's reputation as a poet. The other albums were both entitled* Buch der Liebe *(Book of Love). Marx and Heine became friends in Paris.*

The lantern burns so softly,
And casts a mellow light.
It seems to weep beside me,
As if it knew my plight.

Again it finds me lonely,
And sunk within my breast,
Where ghostly forms of shadow
By fantasy are dressed.

It somehow seems to realise
That its poor guttering part
Will pale before the fire
That burns deep in my heart.

Doch ach! die Gluth, sie ruhet,
Nicht in sich selber mehr,
Es sind nur schwache Strahlen
Aus Deiner Seele Meer.

WIENER AFFENTHEATER IN BERLIN

I

"Ei sagt, das Publikum drängt sich wüthend fort!
Gewiß ein Talma da, ein Musenort!"
Bitt' Freund, man liebt nicht scharfe Waffen,
Komödie ist's, gespielt von – Affen.

II

Ich saß und blickt' in guter Ruh,
Dem reinen Spiel der Bestien zu,
Natur, die war nicht zu vermissen,
Hätt'n nur noch solln an die Wände —.
Da fühlt' ich mich plötzlich am Mantel gepackt:
"Denkt euch, der Streich war ganz vertrackt,
Ein Fräulein ist in Ohnmacht fallen,
Stürzt toll 'nem Affen an Brust und Krallen,
Sie schlug ihr Aug', sie sprach so bang,
O! tiefer Ahndungsseelendrang,
O! Harmonie, o Geisterpein,
Der Affe spielt' mir in's Herz hinein,

But, ah, that fire is fading,
And it can never be.
I only have weak radiance
That shines from your soul's sea.

VIENNESE MONKEY-THEATRE IN BERLIN

In this poem, Marx satirises comic theatre and those who take it too seriously. He writes from a somewhat male point of view. The attack on naturalistic drama does not sit well with Marxist aesthetic theory, as Prawer notes.[12] *François-Joseph Talma, mentioned in line 2, was a famous tragic actor of the period.*

I

"Just look, the public throngs in frenzied queues!
A Talma must be here! Or some such Muse!"
Ah, friend, the weapons used are chunky.
This is comedy, played by the… monkey.

II

I sat and calmly watched the play,
And saw the animals having their way,
And only one small thing was missing:
To watch them at the wall and —.
But then a hand grabbed on my coat:
"My God, that trick was intricate!
A young girl fainted to the floor,
Entranced by monkey breast and claw.
She blinked and said, in sheer duress:
O deep avenging soul-in-stress!
O harmony, o spirit's pain,
The monkey has my heart to gain!

[12] Prawer *op. cit.*, p. 15.

Ich fühle mich magnetisch fortgetrieben,
Der Affe spielt' mich selbst, ich mußt' ihn lieben,
O! sprich, wie kömmst du mich doch für,
Der Hauch versagt, das Auge schwindelt mir.

EPIGRAMME

I

In seinem Sessel, behaglich dumm,
Sitzt schweigend das deutsche Publikum.
Braust der Sturm herüber, hinüber,
Wölkt sich der Himmel düster und trüber,
Zischen die Blitze schlängelnd hin,
Das rührt es nicht in seinem Sinn.
Doch wenn sich die Sonne hervorbeweget,
Die Lüfte säuseln, der Sturm sich leget,
Dann hebt's sich und macht ein Geschrei,
Und schreibt ein Buch: "der Lärm sei vorbei."
Fängt an darüber zu phantasieren,
Will dem Ding auf den Grundstoff spüren,
Glaubt, das sei doch nicht die rechte Art,
Der Himmel spasse auch ganz apart,
Müsse das All systematischer treiben,
Erst an dem Kopf, dann an den Füssen reiben,

Some magnet draws me to new ways!
The monkey plays me on the stage!
O speak, for you have caught my soul!
My breath – it fails! My eyes – they roll!"

EPIGRAMS

Marx had a keen sense of humour that he often used to satirical effect: Francis Wheen reads Capital *as a satire about capitalism in the spirit of Sterne.*[13] *The epigrams below comprise the first two sections of a series of eight.*

I

In this lengthy epigram, Marx takes a swipe against bourgeois philistines who refuse to read the signs of the times. It anticipates his contention that people make their decisions in circumstances determined for them.

In his armchair, cosy and stupid,
Sits silently our German public.
The storm roars closer, the storm roars over,
The clouds get deeper, the clouds get darker,
And lighting hisses like snakes entwined:
But none of this will stir his mind.
Yet when the sun reclaims the sky
And breezes rustle and storm-clouds die,
Then up he gets and gives a scream,
And writes a book: *The Noise Has Been.*
And now he begins to fantasise.
He subjects the Thing to analysis.
His firm belief is that something's not right.
Heaven can make a joke if it likes,
But should make the universe more systematic:
It should rub the head and then rub the feet.

[13] Wheen, *op. cit.*, p. 308.

Gebärd't sich nun gar, wie ein Kind,
Sucht nach Dingen, die vermodert sind,
Hätt' indessen die Gegenwart sollen erfassen,
Und Erd' und Himmel laufen lassen,
Gingen ja doch ihren gewöhnlichen Gang,
Und die Welle braust ruhig den Fels entlang.

II

HEGEL

1

Weil ich das Höchste entdeckt und die Tiefe sinnend gefunden,
Bin ich grob, wie ein Gott, hüll' mich in Dunkel, wie er.
Lange forscht' ich und trieb auf dem wogenden Meer der
Gedanken,
Und da fand ich das Wort, halt' am Gefundenen fest.

2

Worte lehr' ich, gemischt in dämonisch verwirrtem Getriebe,
Jeder denke sich dann, was ihm zu denken beliebt.
Wenigstens ist er nimmer geengt durch fesselnde Schranken,
Denn wie aus brausender Fluth, stürzend vom ragenden Fels,
Sich der Dichter ersinnt der Geliebten Wort und Gedanken,
Und was er sinnet, erkennt, und was er fühlet, ersinnt,
Kann ein jeder sich saugen der Weisheit labenden Nektar,
Alles sag' ich euch ja, weil ich ein Nichts euch gesagt!

Then he starts to take on childish ways
And looks for things from better days,
Instead of grasping hold of the Now
And letting earth and heaven both go
The way they've gone from way, way back.
And softly breaks the wave along the rocks.

II

HEGEL

Marx was deeply influenced by the philosopher Georg Friedrich Wilhelm Hegel, but reacted against his tendency to abstraction.

1

Hegel is made to satirise himself by overblown language in unrhymed elegiac couplets.

As I have found what's on high and have sensed what is down in
  the depths,
I'm as coarse as a God, and shrouded in darkness, like Him.
Long did I search, and I sailed out on thoughts that were surging
  as seas,
And there I found the Word. I hold to what I have found.

2

Another epigram in the same classical form (pioneered in German Literature by Goethe and Schiller). Words can be a cover for saying nothing.

Words do I teach, mixed up and confused, in a demon's true frenzy,
So let everyone think... just what they choose they might think.
At least they are never hemmed in, by shackles of sheer limitation,
For out of the roaring flood, plummeting down from the rock,
So does the poet invent words and thoughts for his own true beloved.
And what he senses, he sees; and what he feels, he invents.
Each can then suck for himself at wisdom's nourishing nectar.
And I've told you all, because I've just told you... nothing!

3

Kant und Fichte gern zum Aether schweifen,
Suchten dort ein fernes Land,
Doch ich such' nur tüchtig zu begreifen,
Was ich – auf der Strasse fand!

4

Verzeiht uns Epigrammendingen,
Wenn wir fatale Weisen singen,
Wir haben uns nach Hegel einstudiert,
Auf sein' Aesthetik noch nicht —.
abgeführt.

3

A direct attack on philosophical abstraction, satirising the philosophers Immanuel Kant and Johann Gottlieb Fichte.

Kant and Fichte like to soar to the aether,
Seeking there a distant land.
But I just seek to be a scholar
Of what I… found upon the ground!

4

Finally, a satire on poetasters who have read Hegel's Aesthetics *without it doing them much good. Theory for Marx must always lead to improved practice.*

Pardon us creatures of epigram,
If we sing tunes that tend to damn.
Hegel has been our education.
Aesthetics still awaits… purgation.

BIOGRAPHICAL NOTES

Karl Marx was born in 1818 in Trier in the Rhineland but spent most of his life as a stateless exile in Paris, Brussels and London, where he died in 1883. He supported himself by journalism and the generosity of others. Marx was involved in setting up and leading radical associations and was an active supporter of the 1848 revolutions, which took him back briefly to his homeland. As a law student, he had dreamed of following a literary career and worked on poems, a novel and a play, before deciding that his future lay elsewhere. Marx's major philosophical works include *The Communist Manifesto, The German Ideology* (both co-authored with Friedrich Engels) and *Capital*. His total output is immense. Some 120 of his poems from the years 1836-7 survive and offer a fascinating glimpse into the mind and times of one of history's great thinkers. The texts in this chapbook have been chosen to represent his work in three areas: engagement with the poetic tropes of the day; poems to his future wife Jenny von Westphalen; satirical verse.

Philip Wilson was born in 1959 in Leeds and lives in Norwich, where he teaches philosophy of religion and philosophy of literature at the University of East Anglia. Academic publications include *Translation after Wittgenstein* (Routledge) and the *Routledge Handbook of Translation and Philosophy* (edited with Piers Rawling). Translations include Simone Weil's play *Venice Saved* (Bloomsbury, with Silvia Caprioglio Panizza) and a selection of early German poetry, *The Bright Rose* (Arc). He is currently translating the poetry of Simone Weil (with Silvia Caprioglio Panizza) and working on a book about the relationship between translation, mysticism and esotericism.